Use Conflict

*"The most important of life's battles is the one we fight daily
in the silent chambers of the soul."*
– DAVID O. MCKAY

Praise for "Use Conflict!"

*"Conflict is unavoidable; resolution and cooperation are achievable;
Dave Gerber offers a different way to think about the subject in* Use Conflict,
*while providing us the tools and sharing his experience to make this journey.
He offers skills and concepts that we can use to immediately change
the way we communicate, lead and live our lives."*
– JACK GATES
President
Gates Associates

*"Business is personal. Getting everyone on the same page
is mission critical. Glue this to your employee handbook. "*
– BURL HAIGWOOD
CEO
The Same Page

"Be kind, for everyone you meet is fighting a hard battle."
– PLATO

U~S~E~ CONFLICT!

ADVANCE YOUR WINNING LIFE

BY DAVE GERBER

Published by Timeless Publishing

www.Timelesspublishing.com

E-mail: info@timelesspublishing.com

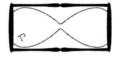

© 2007 by Dave Gerber

ISBN: 978-0-9788707-1-3

Library of Congress Control Number: 2008903875

Second Edition

Printed in the United States of America

Special thanks for the Cover Layout
Designed by Jeff Calabria

Special thanks to Gaye Newton for her editing contributions

Special Thanks to Tony Ford for his cartoon contributions

Acknowledgements

"For it was not into my ear you whispered, but into my heart.
It was not my lips you kissed, but my soul."
                – JUDY GARLAND

I would like to give my deepest recognition, appreciation and love to Kakki and Jessie. Deep thanks to my grandfather, Papa, who was an inspiration to become an author; to my amazingly supportive parents, brother and to my first mentor, Robert Heasley. Also this is to recognize the authentic appreciation for the training and speaking participants I have had the pleasure to address, to say thank you for the great sharing and feelings of success you have helped to create and share throughout my life. I love you all. – DAVE GERBER

"Silent gratitude isn't much use to anyone."
                – GLADYS BROWYN STERN

Table of Contents

*"We are enslaved by anything we do not consciously see.
We are freed by conscious perception."*
– Vernon Howard

Foreword

Much has been written about conflict, yet so much remains unknown. Further, learning more about it or even dealing with conflict does not necessarily help us to better understand its origins, its impact or its consequences – let alone develop a conflict management mentality. We all deal with it every day in one form or another but we tend to continuously struggle with it as a subject. Conflict has been part of our daily lives since we were born and we have all formed our habits, default behaviors and reflex responses in addressing it in all its forms – but the struggle continues.

It's not a pleasant experience and more often than not, it's one of the great causes of distress in our lives. It affects us in our workplace, our family life and certainly in our most important and intimate one-on-one relationships. Why then, are we not working harder to improve our response to this fact of life? In this book, Dave Gerber helps us understand the answer to that and many more challenging questions about the world of conflict.

Through the unique approach of addressing what the author calls the "essential questions," about conflict and the application of F.A.C.T.S. (Fear, Anger, Control, Trust and Synergy), we are guided through a constructive process to help us think more clearly about the subject. He helps us identify, analyze, and understand the key elements of conflict and most importantly, he leaves us with "actionable" means to improve our individual response to the conflicts we face daily. He reminds us of the importance of self-reflection, accepting responsibility, acting courageously, and learning from our experiences. He encourages us to *embrace* conflict and use the conflict that exists to improve the current situation and prepare us for the future. Consider this – we can acknowledge that we can't always avoid it or deny it (not usually good practices, anyway) – and we are taught to USE it in a constructive and collaborative way. For all of us that seem to find conflict without even looking for it, this is most valuable and reassuring.

– DAVID. S. MAURER, LT. COL., USA (RET.)
Vice President
Axiom Resource Management, Inc.

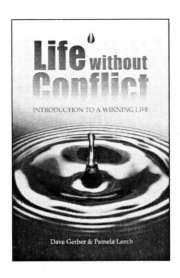

www.lifewithoutconflict.com

Life without Conflict: Introduction to a Winning Life is my first book, written with a friend and co-author Pamela Leech. *Use Conflict: Advance Your Winning Life* represents the next step, one that I believe builds upon some of the concepts originally explored in our first book and introduces new ones not previously discussed. These two books, while they sound contradictory, work together to build the bridge between conflict theory and practice from a different perspective than previously explored by other experts. While at first we want to believe that we can get rid of all conflict, we soon realize that is impossible and need to use it. These books also stand alone as personal guides on the subject of conflict and can help in their own way to make conflict something that is less intimidating and something that can be *used* to our personal satisfaction, growth and forward progress.

<u>USE</u> CONFLICT!

ADVANCE YOUR WINNING LIFE
BY DAVE GERBER

Preface

"You cannot run away from a weakness; you must sometimes fight it out or perish. And if that be so, why not now, and where you stand?"
– LOUIS STEVENSON

Why *Use Conflict?*

Conflict is inevitable, so we should *use it*. Moving beyond the understanding that conflict is inevitable forces us to make a plan to use it, whether that is in the form of prevention, management or resolution practices and skills. Our ability to use our conflict fluency and prevention tools—through repetition, less self-judgment and the pursuit of actualizing a better, bigger self—we can choose to overcome and use obstacles as milestones for our growth and improved daily life.

What is a Winning Life?

In a winning life, things feel as if they are moving forward. We are learning, growing from our mistakes, and being less judgmental of ourselves and others. We feel large and feel empowered when sharing experiences. Our predominant emotional state is positive, and we can catch ourselves in negative self-talk and turn it around. We are authentic and present, and we understand our purpose for getting out of bed in the morning. We have the love, motivation and energy to do it. This winning life is possible for all of us.

It takes daily work and a never ending pursuit of happiness, fulfillment, actualization of our true selves, belief in the possibilities, more hard work, taking the time to appreciate others, support and through ritualizing ongoing successes. Really, just imagine!

Conflict Cartoons

A unique twist has been added to this by including "Humorous Political Style" cartoons at the end of each chapter. While the goal is to lighten the subject of conflict and increase reading pleasure, it is vitally important to understand the quotes used are also intended as insightful hints to help us. Please read the caption and then enjoy the picture while transitioning to the next chapter.

Everything that irritates us about others can lead us to an understanding of ourselves.
- Carl Gustav Jung

I.
Critical Conflict Questions

"I beg you...to have patience with everything unresolved in your heart and try to love the questions themselves as if they were locked rooms or books written in a very foreign language. Don't search for the answers, which could not be given you now, because you would not be able to live them. And the point is, to live everything. Live the questions now. Perhaps then, someday far in the future, you will gradually, without every noticing it, live your way into the answer..."
— Rainer Maria Rilke

There are several critical questions that offer vital information on the subject of conflict, much of which we should know up front. These questions and answers represent a skeleton to a thorough understanding of conflict. The goal is to highlight, in the form of essential questions, information that lies at the heart of using conflict to our advantage. It is also a goal to motivate us to want to read more, as we can quickly see how a few changes can create a new lifetime reality.

It is often helpful to consider that when we take the time to slow down, listen and learn, we often find that our desire to investigate ourselves grows stronger than our fear of being wrong. The following are 11 Critical Conflict Questions that force us to further investigate the conflict in our lives.

Critical Question Overview

1. What is conflict?

2. How do we use conflict?

3. Who gets emotionally hijacked?

4. What is Default Behavior?

5. What role does judgment have in our lives?

6. What is the difference between conflict prevention, management and resolution?

7. What really happens when we make assumptions?

8. How can we avoid conflict when giving feedback?

9. Why should we understand Interest-Based Problem Solving?

10. What is the difference between reacting and responding?

11. Why should we investigate this subject even further?

1. What is Conflict?

Conflict occurs when anything or anyone gets in the way of something we truly want or threatens the way we want to be or how we want to move through an experience. More formal definitions include concepts like open clashes between groups or opposition between two simultaneous but incompatible feelings. Conflict can be viewed as a state of opposition between persons or ideas or interests, or a disagreement or argument about something important.[1]

Limited time or resources are just two examples of variables that can limit our ability to have our desires met. This can cause immediate conflicting thoughts, feelings, and behaviors. Consider any number of times we have needed more time or money to complete a project to our standard.

We choose how we react to what other people say or do. Many people choose to engage in or escalate conflict, rather than move slowly and make decisions based on the outcomes they need. Two revealing questions are, "What is my predominant emotional state of mind?" and "What moods do I find myself in most of the time?" This encourages a whole set of considerations that can lead to a greater understanding of how to use conflict as an opportunity for learning, growth, increased performance, revenue generation, and risk reduction.

Conflict often happens when we face roadblocks, fixate on our positions instead of interests, lack the desire to understand before we are understood, do not see other perspectives, refuse to truly listen or allow the pains of our past experiences—even as far back as childhood—to dominate our present reality.

Society has not truly embraced and taught the value of using conflict as a means to move something forward, build new relationships, or complete a project. Conflict may be absolutely necessary for people to move forward together.

2. How Do We Use Conflict?

We can use conflict by increasing our understanding of the subject and by working each day to prevent, manage and resolve it to our advantage. Conflict can often be predicted, anticipated and prevented. When it's not expected, we can manage the environment, people, resources, and other variables to increase the likelihood of a positive outcome.

Using conflict is truly about blending skills and attitude about the conflict that exists in our everyday lives. It is about an approach towards building skills and life experiences that help us when faced with similar obstacles or situations. We can see conflict as a source of something with great potential for learning and growth in relationships and in life.

In order to use conflict, we must understand that it is both positive and negative. We're all familiar with negative conflict. It can:
- Create more conflict.
- Eliminate "response ability."
- Create physiological responses that impede our ability to make sound, cognitive, logical decisions.

- Sabotage decision making.
- Undermine creativity.
- Re-emphasize our past poor decision making.
- Trigger our default behavior that creates more conflict.
- Cause anxiety, mental and physical stress and/or sickness.
- Annihilate respect and trust.
- Impede our ability to move forward internally or with others.
- Create war.

Positive conflict, however, may often be the only way to proactively deal with issues that people or groups need to have addressed. Conflict can be the beginning of a great thing or the ending of something that needs closure. It can:

- Be the start to something new.
- Initiate change.
- Be the end to something that needs closure.
- Positively redirect something off track.
- Use diversity.
- Promote understanding.
- Support dialogue.
- Enlighten someone that is unaware of a problem.
- Be the start of something unexpected.
- Become a life-long learning opportunity.
- Foster self-esteem.
- Reinforce our current abilities, strengths or contributions.
- Help work to ensure life-long happiness.

But even though it is positive, it may not be easy or painless to manage. Creating a mentality that promotes using conflict will help to avoid the costly and difficult by-product of negative conflict.

Positive conflict, by its very nature, can signal a moment to explore perspectives, look at common interests, open lines of communication, generate learning opportunities and help us separate the people from the problem.

We far too often see people react to conflict with anger, avoidance, fear, guilt, shame, procrastination or complete shut down. But it is equally possible for individuals to choose positive thinking and to brainstorm and produce new perspectives, ideas and even a new road map or dynamic. The process can strengthen character and reinforce how we view and ultimately use conflict to our advantage.

3. Who Gets Emotionally Hijacked?

At times, almost everyone can get *emotionally hijacked* — experience a changing physiological state where blood pressure increases and chemicals are released in the brain limiting the ability to think creatively and logically.

When you have a panic attack, or become very anxious your emotional response can actually bypass your "thinking brain." The... amygdala [small but powerful part of the brain], which is involved with creating a "faster than thought" panic attack... [gets triggered]. It is very difficult, or impossible, to think clearly when highly emotional because the part of the brain you think with is inhibited...This response has been termed an "emotional hijacking" by Daniel Goleman.[2]

One can think of this phenomenon as the *inverse* of "being in the zone." We have heard of blinding rage or have been so frustrated that we couldn't really make rational decisions or see straight. Goleman and most other researchers in the field agree that when this phenomenon happens, the feeling can last a minimum of 10 minutes.

Consider all of the things our brain is responsible for—logic, reason, breathing, decision making, creativity, communication, etc. When we are really angry and get hijacked, many of those functions get disrupted. When this happens, we have lost our ability to work with other people to find solutions that satisfy everyone. We have essentially lost our minds!

We are responsible for our behavior, whether we are hijacked or not. When reactions do not pass acceptable standards, consequences generally follow. Even if responses from others are not vocalized, witnessing someone that is emotionally hijacked is difficult to forget or even overcome.

Emotional hijacking can escalate the negativity in a relationship or situation. While we are not responsible for other people's feelings, we do contribute to them and often make it easier for people to get frustrated. Language is powerful. People under stressful situations can be sensitive. A single word may be a bridge to more conflict if we are not careful.

4. What is Default Behavior?

Default behavior describes the set of behaviors we fall back to when things get difficult—patterns that we repeat without even considering what we are doing or its impact. Here are a few examples from a colleague, Karen, and her self-reported default behaviors:

When I feel...	Fear	Anger	Control	Shame	Guilt
My default behavior is to...	Run	Fight	Leave Temporarily	Apologize	Submit

Other examples:
- When team members disagree over objectives, each person immediately heads for his or her cubicle.
- When a couple fights, he goes to the bedroom and slams the door, while she goes to the local bar.
- When he feels out of control, he cleans.
- When he gets angry, he fires off mean e-mails to subordinates.

Default behaviors can very easily dominate our reactions, moods or behaviors when conflict happens. The impact of our social learning, the lessons from our parents and our formal and informal training (the Agents of Socialization, discussed in Chapter 3), directly impact the speed at which we fall into our negative patterns. A person may unknowingly move into autopilot mode and seem to be acting from patterned, default behavior.

In order for us to change these default behaviors and be more successful when conflict arises, we need to observe ourselves when triggered. We need to break the pattern by changing our actions. It is important to recognize and try to catch ourselves in the moment. When we have failed to do so, we should release judgment and work towards a better outcome the next time. Hopefully we do not owe anyone an apology. If so, we offer one and try to move forward.

5. What Role Does Judgment Have in Our Lives?

If we really pay attention, it seems that judgment has become sewn into the very fabric of our self talk and the way we treat one another. In the workplace or in the home, we often get trapped in the negativity that can trigger cyclical messages in our head. Judgment is reported to be one of our top fears as human beings.

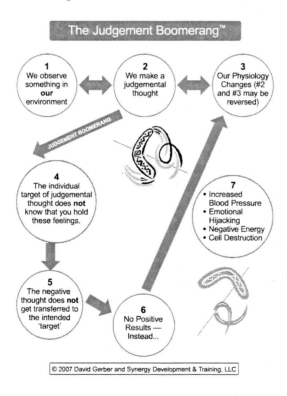

The Judgement Boomerang™

1. We observe something in **our** environment

2. We make a judgemental thought

3. Our Physiology Changes (#2 and #3 may be reversed)

4. The individual target of judgemental thought does **not** know that you hold these feelings.

5. The negative thought does **not** get transferred to the intended 'target'

6. No Positive Results — Instead...

7. • Increased Blood Pressure • Emotional Hijacking • Negative Energy • Cell Destruction

© 2007 David Gerber and Synergy Development & Training, LLC

If we truly examine the impact of a judgmental thought, it usually hurts us physiologically or even spiritually more than it hurts the intended target.

6. What is the Difference between Conflict Prevention, Management and Resolution?

Imagine someone trying to cover a wound with a bandage. The bleeding may stop for a brief moment with direct pressure. Could it have been easier to prevent the accident in the first place? Could that individual have chosen to wear a long sleeve shirt or a jacket, maybe some gloves, before hiking through the wilderness?

Our society does not want to think about, or spend the resources to prevent conflict from happening before it starts. Consider crime. If we asked a group of parents if they would be interested in more police officers, emergency and/or fire personnel, most would say yes. If we then told them how much their taxes would need to increase to support the approved initiative, most would rationalize a way to say, "Everything is truly okay and nothing happens around here, so, no, I won't support it."

Taking the time, energy, resources and money to prevent conflict before it starts is the only way to ensure that we are as prepared as we can be when conflict rears its head. Human beings equal conflict. If we believe this, we can believe that preventing conflict is smart and rational and will affect our professional and personal lives. (Whoever said that business isn't personal wasn't looking beyond his or her experience.)

Conflict prevention incorporates a wide range of thoughts, planning, actions and follow-up that creates informal and formal policies, procedures and practice, all with a clear and established purpose known as the 4-P State of Mind.

This theory is used to describe the expectations courts of law will have on a company or organization. First, there must be *policies*. Secondly, we must examine the *purpose* of the policy in order to make sure that it is correctly stated and clear to all. Then the policies must have appropriate and clear *procedures* about how to follow those policies or what to do if a policy is broken. Finally, just like fire drills, procedures must be *practiced*. Everyone, both new hires and those who have been working for a while, needs a refresher course.

Think about it. Would it be acceptable for a school to have a fire policy but only practice it every other year? No. Policies and procedures must be put to the test and practiced. The end goal is to avert the problem or at least reduce the escalation and/or damage involved.

Conflict prevention **includes:**

1. Engaging in self-assessment, monitoring, and positive self-talk that will allow us to avert or manage a potentially disruptive conflict. Self-talk is widely viewed as the little internal discussions that, during quiet times, we have with ourselves about our lives.
2. Understanding the Agents of Socialization and other root causes directly related to the conflict at hand.
3. Understanding our own buttons or default behaviors enough to warn ourselves of an impending conflict and/or a potentially harmful reaction.
4. Developing a prevention-oriented mindset that understands, anticipates and proactively considers the impact of conflict in each area of personal and professional life.
5. Ensuring ourselves and those around us that we are dedicated to strengthening our skills and preventing conflict in every aspect of life.

Conflict prevention addresses a desire to gain the appropriate tools and skills. But this new learning is only made useful when it is applied fairly and consistently with great reflection.

Conflict management is about using a conflict prevention mentality and working toward resolution, self-awareness and a system or procedure for immediately dealing with conflict. Our goal is to prevent the initiation of conflict, quickly facilitate a method for containment when it happens and enable ourselves to transform the experience into solutions, calmness, growth and life-long learning.

Conflict resolution is a method or process of extinguishing or handling a conflict, preferably quickly, by:

- Identifying the main, secondary, tertiary and related issues.
- Addressing each side's or our own internal competing needs.
- Adequately addressing personal and professional interests.
- Investigating unmet professional expectations.
- Understanding and anticipating the possible consequences of any decision (cause and effect).
- Allowing for the customized design of solutions between the parties involved in conflict.

- Including all appropriate individuals and stake holders.
- Staying solution oriented.
- Creating a plan, making choices and confirming the outcomes.
- Developing a plan for honest, effective feedback.
- Actively listening to all parties involved, without interruption.
- Resolving issues through arbitration, mediation, negotiation, alternative dispute resolution or a court of law.

The more we focus on conflict prevention, the less conflict we will have to manage and resolve. Each of these stages is a part of the process of transforming conflict into an agent for positive change. For instance, the identification and elimination of the conditions that fuel conflict support prevention. Management is appropriate when conflict, as positive change, is critical for achieving the desired results. Resolution encompasses prevention and management, resulting in a paradigm shift and win-win solutions for all parties involved.

7. What Really Happens When We Make Assumptions?

When we make assumptions, we instantaneously create, or spin, or own version of the story. We generate feelings from that story and often take action, even if it is just changing the way we think or feel about something or someone and nothing is done in the outside world. The following chart[3] truly demonstrates how quickly we go through the assumption process. We can all think of multiple times a day, if we are truly self critical, that we do this.

one person:	I act
	I draw on beliefs and make conclusions
	I make assumptions
	I add my meaning
	I filter and select pieces of information
	I view or experience an event -- perspective

8. How Can We Avoid Conflict When Giving Feedback?

There are several ways that we can avoid conflict when we provide feedback. Conflict often arises because we have not considered and/or practiced the following principles.

It is critical to begin discussions with positive or disarming statements. No one wants to speak to someone that starts out with a negative statement, question or comment. Considering the other person's needs or interests, the past relationship, the purpose for speaking and expected outcomes, we add the Positive – Negative – Positive model to our overall approach:

Mike: "Thanks for turning off the TV to speak with me."

Sally: "Sure."

Mike: "I wanted to speak with you about what you said to me last night about not expressing my feelings enough."

Sally: "Okay."

Mike: "First, I appreciate that you are interested in how I feel and that you respect me enough to ask when I do not outright share." (Positive)

"In the future when you ask me to share, and I am not ready or have nothing to say, could you not continue to ask me what's wrong or to tell you how I feel?" (Negative)

"As I said, I really do appreciate your checking in with me about how I feel because just the fact that you ask means you are thinking about me." (Positive)

The feedback for Sally is much easier to hear and reduces the likelihood of emotional and physiological distress. It is also more of a discussion starter, whereby Sally can ask for good ways to express this interest, and maybe, even a neutral code word that is an indicator for her to step back a little.

Another way to give feedback is to use an acronym commonly accepted in the field of training and consulting: F.O.R.M.S. It stands for Factual, Observable, Reliable, Measurable and Specific.[4]

Factual

When we give feedback, we collect all relevant data and facts (and even some unrelated information if it can be helpful) before entering into a discussion. Greater conflict often comes from acting, reacting or giving feedback based on inaccuracies.

Observable

We include observable behaviors related to the issue at hand. It may not be acceptable to respond to an issue that we have not ever witnessed from first-person perspective. It brings credibility to our communication when the other individual knows that we have observed the issue at hand.

Reliable

Consistency and trustworthiness are critical when providing feedback.

Measurable

We use established, predetermined ways to assess and gauge performance levels. Measurement should not be seen as an extra when providing feedback, training or professional development.

Specific

Feedback that is not specific will only create resentment, more questions and conflict. Telling someone, "It isn't good enough" or "You could have done it better" does nothing for either party other than increase frustration and inefficiency.

While we're on the topic, here are a few other things to consider:

Eye Contact

Eye contact is cultural and should be viewed with sensitivity to intercultural expectations. Assuming culture is not the issue, direct eye contact without a break can be intimidating. Eyes are a powerful weapon in the workplace and should not be underestimated. The type of eye contact we give will often determine much of the response we get back.

Body Language

Albert Mehrabian, Professor Emeritus of Psychology at UCLA, conducted a famous study used by thousand of trainers. According to him, over 55 percent of our communication with someone involves our body language. Only 38 percent involves tone of voice, and only seven percent is verbal).

Body language can be considered either open or closed. Crossed arms say, "closed," for example, and can be perceived as negative. It is important that we not let negative body language completely get in the way. We may be misunderstanding signals and begin to get frustrated on an assumption. After all, crossed arms can also mean, "I'm cold." The physical environment impacts body language, energy and connectivity. Is there a physical obstacle in the path, such as a desk, that may represent a true hindrance to communication?

Currency

Everyone has something that motivates him or her. For some it is money, for others it is validation, respect, or vacation time. Here are some examples:

- Trust or respect
- Money
- Validation
- Responsibility

If we know the type of currency someone values, we will know better how to deal our feedback.

9. Why Should We Understand Interest-Based Problem Solving?

Good things happen when we stop focusing on where we are and focus on where we need and want to be when the conflict is over. When we believe that a solution is possible, even if one is not clear at the moment, we are more likely to create successful outcomes.

As noted by Ury and Fisher in their book, *Getting to Yes*, positions are predetermined solutions or outcomes to a situation, conflict or problem. They represent feelings and thoughts about where we are grounded (stuck) and are usually only solved with a single answer, most often a discussion stopper.

For example, if a couple is planning a vacation, the discussion might sound like this:
"I want to go to Bermuda."
"I want to go to Orlando."
"I want to go to Bermuda."
"I want to go to Orlando."

How long can these two have a discussion like this without creating more conflict? Both have taken a position, a predetermined outcome, before actually speaking with one another.

Interests are the underlying needs—not necessarily victory—behind the positions that must be met to feel satisfied. These represent feelings and thoughts about where we want to be and open the box for customized solutions and new conversations.[5]

Following the example above, if we were to ask the partners their reasons for choosing that particular destination, we might learn something fascinating. He wants to go to Bermuda for good golf and restaurants and to be near the beach. She wants to go to Orlando for good restaurants, to be near the beach and to have Disney Land for the kids. During conflict, when we look further into interests, we often find that both individuals actually have many similar, overlapping needs.

Understanding and using interest-based conflict management styles in our lives allows us to move beyond difficult situations with others. This is a beneficial and healthy transition from our old, social learning. Most K-12 school systems, colleges, universities and graduate schools do not teach this type of thinking or problem solving. It has been taken by the negotiation world. But we should all practice this thinking to even have a chance at a winning life.

This is one of the most important elements for us to capture as we move through these pages. People often stick to their positions because they are angry, hurt, or feeling unheard. Yet these emotions get in the way of win-win solutions that create desired outcomes for both parties based upon underlying, spoken or unspoken needs.

When we enter into conflict focused on resolution that satisfies only our own needs, we tend to resort to protecting our positions, feelings and thoughts. But if we can focus on criteria that meet both parties' interests, the solution will be more acceptable to both and often not as confrontational.

Asking the question, "What do you need?" focuses us on interests and needs and allows us to concentrate on why a particular solution is preferred. It generates explanations, not justification. Negative energy is similar to feeling backed into a corner. So we think about ways to let people explain themselves rather than justify their behavior or decision-making. Working with a forward thinking, customized, flexible approach allows for a greater success rate.

Modeled after Uri and Fischer's work, the following diagram on page 19 demonstrates one way to create a pre-planning guide for difficult conversations. Best practices demonstrate that the most effective communicators can shift the dynamic, remove some of the situational tension and demonstrate genuine interest in the other party's needs. After mutually acceptable outcomes have been generated, both parties should individually reflect on the content, outcome and process of the conversation in order to improve the next one.

The benefits of the time taken to prepare and complete this form are numerous. When dealing with long term solutions, conflict or communication issues, it is best to be prepared. The following guide will help individuals feel more comfortable with the ambiguity of conflict and isolated situations. The steps to the model include:

Predetermined Outcomes

Happy or sad, right or wrong, good or bad, this is the outcome someone has in their head prior to the discussion taking place. Consider someone putting a stake in the ground. It is specific, definite and usually not a discussion starter.

To use an earlier example, if a couple were going to discuss vacation plans, each might come into the discussion somewhat hard headed, only wanting to go to either Bermuda or Orlando. Imagine two people only discussing, probably forcibly, the merits of their predetermined vacation outcome.

Underlying Needs

Everyone has underlying needs that drive predetermined outcomes. For example:
- Respect
- Validation
- Recognition
- Money
- Family
- Promotion/advancement

Disarming Technique

The ability to diffuse conflict before it starts is a critical element when giving feedback. Demonstrating empathy right at the beginning of a conversation, for example, may disarm someone's anger, disappointment or frustration level. If the underlying interests of the other party can be considered, it is possible to diffuse at the beginning of a discussion. Individuals brace for conflict. This technique will help encourage the person to relax and want to hear more, as they now do not have to fight the original conflict.

Consider these common underlying needs to use as part of the framework for our first substantive words when having difficult conversations:
- Respect (e.g., "Before we continue, I want you to know that the company respects the quality of your work.")
- Recognition
- Validation
- Promotion/advancement
- Accountability
- Meet the mission or complete the objectives
- Money
- Family
- Loyalty
- Increased communication and feedback

It is vitally important to understand that this statement must be transparent, genuine, and appropriate for the discussion, relationship, context of the situation and more. Any opening disarming statement that is misinterpreted as not being truthful, honest, or respectful will ultimately end up igniting more conflict. Here are a few examples of disarming statements:

- Apologies
- Statements of accountability
- Inquiries about family members (extremely sensitive one to use)
- Statements of respect
- Statements of appreciation
- Statements about increased feedback or communication
- Statements about loyalty or desire to support

Plan B

This is a concrete backup plan that is the best, worst alternative to an agreement. It is something that can be actualized if the other party is unwilling to collaborate. It must be real, and it must be possible to follow up with it immediately. The ability to generate a backup plan prior to engaging in difficult conversations gives us choices. While we must be careful not to live a self-fulfilling prophecy or become negative, we do need to have options. Not everything is negotiable. Here are a few examples:

- Quit
- File a grievance
- File an EEO complaint
- Go outside of the chain of command
- Leave

Potential Outcomes

Potential outcomes are created with the other party in joint brainstorming and discussions. It is recommended to brainstorm individually prior to the discussion in order to demonstrate preparation, empathy and that we are solution oriented.

The greatest part about potential outcomes and engaging in this process is that individuals can come together to do more than they could on their own. Parties can create possibilities and solutions that are customized within the boundaries of law, rules, regulations and precedence, yet have been crafted to meet the needs of both parties.

Third Party Criteria

Third party criteria are rules or guidelines placed upon us by someone or an organization greater than ourselves. They dictate how creative we can be with our solutions and help us to reality test our results and sometimes remove the emotion from the equation. Here are a few examples:

- Kelly Blue Book
- Comparisons on a house
- Rules, regulations or laws
- Historical precedents

Solutions and Reflections

The research shows us on many fronts, in many industries, with multiple studies, that the most successful individuals are the ones that not only come to win-win solutions and meet the needs of both parties, they engage in the reflection process once the decisions are made.

After decisions are made, the most successful negotiators reflect on personal verbal and non-verbal behavior, strategy, questioning techniques, the quality of listening. They determine whether they need to change anything in the future.

By using this the following form to prepare for a negotiation, difficult conversation or conflict, we can be more prepared to disarm the conflict and move to individual and mutual needs.

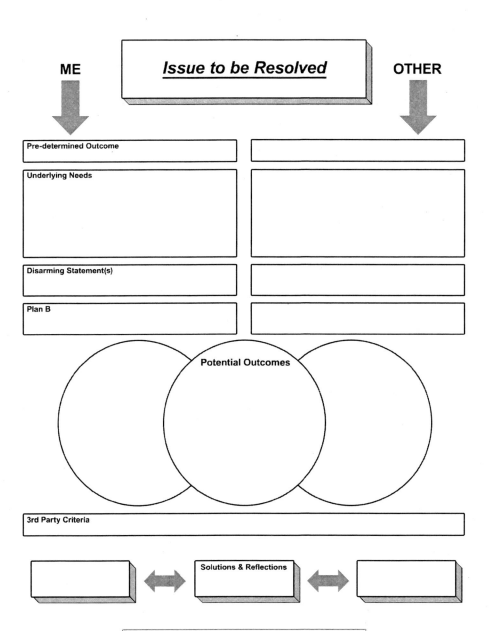

ME

OTHER

Issue to be Resolved

Pre-determined Outcome

Underlying Needs

Disarming Statement(s)

Plan B

Potential Outcomes

3rd Party Criteria

Solutions & Reflections

SYNERGY PLANNING GUIDE -- Synergy Development & Training, LLC © 2007

10. What Is The Difference Between Reacting And Responding?

Reacting vs. Responding

We live in a society that is very reactive and fearful. People often feel defensive. No one likes to be judged or forced to explain why they did or did not do something.

The important distinction between reacting and responding is critical. Most of us react because we have not trained our brains to slow down. When we slow down in conflict, our brains have time to become flooded with options. This means we are actively choosing a response, rather than allowing an internal, emotional or physical change to dictate how we will speak or behave.

Reacting is a sudden, immediate internal or external action or feeling that contains lots of emotion and, quite often, no consideration of how it will affect us or others. *Responding* means to slow down and select a path, decision or behavior while considering the action itself, the people affected and the possible consequences.

The Reptilian Reaction describes how humans respond automatically to positive or negative events without consciously thinking about the consequences. It is grounded in emotion, not logic. Derived from the theory of the reptilian brain, this teaching principle describes the sequence of events in a cause and effect relationship. It claims that the primitive (reptilian) part of the brain controls lust, fear, hate and love. When we react, we are actually operating with this primitive part, using emotion over logic and reason.

Reptiles and other animals do this instinctively. So do people who have not been taught to slow down and consider their immediate and long term actions and consequences. Usually the choice of reactive behavior is not a conscious choice at all. Rather, it is a reaction that perpetuates negativity and often creates a cycle of conflict that spirals out of control.

People often resort to this behavior when their coping skills are limited or they cannot see other options. They stick with the approaches that they are most comfortable with and experienced in using. But once they are consciously aware of how they feel, they can make a better choice.

While it is easy to believe that we are responding to the events in our lives, our feelings in the moment are related to our immediate, internalized interpretations and preconceived notions about the event. Therefore, the way we interpret events will often dictate our response or Reptilian Reaction.

There are several ways to avoid reacting and control decision making:
1. Understand our own emotions.
    • Understand the causes of our feelings.
    • Become aware of our hot buttons.
    • Develop frustration tolerance.
    • Strengthen our sense of self worth and reduce our dependence on external validation.
2. Recognize the isolated action.
3. Stop—do not react—and breathe.
    • Avoid thinking in terms of extremes.
    • Avoid believing that our perspective is the only one that exists.
    • Do not over generalize or blow things out of proportion.
    • Do not personalize the entire conflict.
    • Do not allow this experience to overshadow our successes.
4. Ask ourselves if it is possible that we misinterpreted what they said, or they misinterpreted us.
5. Step into the space of "now."
6. Acknowledge options, impact, and consequences.
    (What are my options for expressing my feelings?)
7. Select a response using logic over emotion.
8. Stated another way:
    • Identify the action or behavior.
    • Step willingly and knowingly into the space.
    • Identify potential responses.
    • Identify the consequences and impact of each option.
    • Knowingly choose a response based upon a conscious decision.

"A life of reaction is a life of slavery, intellectually and spiritually. One must fight for a life of action, not reaction."
– RITA MAE BROWN

11. Why Should We Investigate This Subject Further Now?

- To live a more fulfilled life now, for as long as possible.
- To improve our ability to handle ambiguity.
- To be able to help others improve their life immediately.
- To improve our personal and professional relationships quickly and with a lasting impact.
- To increase the quality of interactions between strangers and acquaintances.
- To improve our understanding of why conflict exists, how it impacts our lives and how to prevent it from happening in the future.
- To develop a stronger conflict fluency that will help us dissect conflict in the moment and handle it in way that limits emotional reactions.
- To help create the best solutions as our physiology changes while in conflict.
- To further develop new tools to understand and deal with the quickly changing world around us.

1 <wordnet.princeton.edu/perl/webwn> (October 1, 2007).

2 Panic-attacks.co.uk, "Part 5: The Brain and Panic Attacks: Emotional Hijacking," *The Panic Attack Prevention Program*, 2001-2006, <http://www.panic-attacks.co.uk/panic_attacks_5.htm/> (July 26, 2006.)

3 Modified from Art Kelner, Peter Senge, Richard Ross, Bryan Smith and Charolotte Roberts, *The Fifth Discipline Field Book*, Currency Doubleday, New York, 1994, p. 243.

4 (original creator unknown).

5 Robert Fischer, William Ury, and Patton, Bruce, *Getting to Yes: Negotiating Agreement without Giving In*, Penguin Group, New York, NY, 1981, pp. 40-41.

Change is inevitable,
growth is optional.
- Walt Disney

II.
"Conflict Fluency" Glossary

"Communication works for those who work at it."
– JOHN POWELL

While some people might believe the following words belong in a glossary, these *critical* concepts and definitions need not be lost to the back part of the book that many people often do not read. These words, phrases and concepts are critical to advancing a winning life and managing and using conflict. Please also examine Appendix A for other critical words and phrases that must be understood to truly manage conflict effectively.

Perception

Our perception is our reality. When something happens, we attach our own personal interpretations to the event, often without hesitation. Like it or not, this perspective is a bias, the effect of our collective, real and imagined life experiences. If our perception is reality, simply, everyone in society is operating under the rules of the reality they have established. Someone once alluded that the only false perception is the one that claims to be the only perception that exists at all.

When conflict happens, one way to begin the diffusion process is to consider someone else's perspective, even if they are not involved in the situation. How might she or he see it differently? How can our ability to look from another perspective impact our ability to shift the dynamic and find temporary or permanent solutions?

But

Avoid this word whenever possible. When someone uses the word it in conversation, a number of things happen:
- The speaker feels interrupted and/or negated.
- The speaker wonders if he or she has truly been heard.
- The speaker wonders if the listener has processed the newly presented information.
- The speaker wonders if the listener was only looking for the first opportunity to discuss his or her own issues.
- The speaker may be offended at the negative transition.
- The listener may be trying to change the power dynamic or gain some situational control.
- The listener may not realize his or her word selection may be offensive.
- It may set a standard for communicating.
- It can damage the long term relationship.

Substituting But:
- Use "and" instead of "but."
- Consider ending the reflective sentence and starting a new one.
- Ask a good open-ended question about his or her thought.

Why

What happens when we back a skunk into a corner? What happens when we back a human into a corner? In both instances we get sprayed with something.

When we ask "why," we are inherently forcing someone to justify instead of explain him- or herself. There is a very clear distinction between "why" and other words that elicit the same information, particularly as it relates to the potential physiological change for both parties involved.

The person who is justifying him- or herself has an immediate physical change. But the other individual will often subconsciously match that energy level, the language, tone and/or non-verbal behavior.

Substituting Why

We can get to the why without saying it and without using language that makes people defensive. How can the words "who," "what," "where," "when" and "how" be combined into open-ended questions so that more information will surface?

Of the top recognized fears in the U. S., the first five truly have to do with the fear of being judged. Remember:
Required Justification + Fear of Judgment = Disaster!

WIIMF

This is known to many as the "What's in it for me?" principal. We should consider this when trying to create solutions with others, motivate, lead or manage behavior. Everyone wants to have his or her own personal needs met. This is a nice little reminder when we are working to prevent or solve conflict in the moment.

W.A.I.T.

Silence. One way to move from reacting to responding is to remember this helpful acronym: W.A.I.T. (Why Am I Talking?) Am I talking to:
- Defend
- Assert power or control
- Defy
- Problem solve
- Argue a point
- Vent
- Justify
- Explain
- Direct
- Redirect

Allowing for this silence can help ourselves and others:
- Create solutions.
- Understand the ramifications of question/behavior.
- Allow for mutual processing time.
- Allow for a more thought out response.

- Avoid impulsively reacting.
- Demonstrate listening and respect.
- Change the dynamic.

We can use silence to help our brains flood with options that, in turn, allow for a carefully crafted response, rather than a reaction. Creating this space also creates an opportunity for us to fill the void, answer our own questions, begin to construct a solution and so on. Many people are uncomfortable with this pause. It can become just one more people management skill that helps to create win-win solutions.

Open vs. Closed Questions

A colleague of mine, Michelle Wexler, told me this joke and set of teaching points. A man walks into a bar and approaches the bartender. Before the man can speak, the bartender pulls a gun. The man pauses, says thank you, turns and leaves the bar.

Imagine that when inquiring about this situation, only closed questions were permitted. What would it sound like?
- Was it a water gun?   No.
- Did the man know the guy?   No.
- Was it a real gun?   Yes.
- Did the man try to rob the bar? No.
- Was the bar open?   Yes.
- This could go on forever?   Yes.

This seems like a logical progression. How long would we be here if we could only use closed questions? Forever. But if we were permitted to use open ended questions, what would it sound like?
- Why did the man say thank you?
  The man walked into the bar and up to the bartender who noticed he had the hiccups. The bartender pulled a gun from behind the bar and scared the man. The man paused, said thank you, and walked out.

While this is a silly story, we can learn from it. We ask closed questions often because we don't want the answer, don't want the extended version of the answer, don't know what the answer might be, or don't want to deal with ambiguity.

When we use open questions, we choose to dive into the world of ambiguity, which is, for most people, uncomfortable. While lawyers are taught not to ask questions they do not know the answers to, this philosophy will not work in the familial, working and ambiguous world we live in every day.

For example, at the end of writing a book, the author says to his wife, "Did you like the book?" His wife might say, "Yes, I liked the book, yet I didn't like the acknowledgements page, and we could have found a better picture for you." If the author is not prepared to hear this, it might truly have a negative impact. If the he wants to avoid this type of question (and ultimately good helpful data, information and thoughts), he might instead ask, "Do you want to go celebrate my book sales?" But he would miss a valuable opportunity.

We must get more comfortable with ambiguity (i.e., become more comfortable with conflict) so that truth or people's feelings and thoughts can be used for the positive, not emotionally tie us down.

Stop, Start, Continue

- What should we start?
- What should we stop?
- What should we continue?

Synergy Questions

- What do you need, now?
- What is going well?
- What is not going well?
- What do we need to fix?
- How will we fix it?
- What do we need as follow up?

To vs. With

How are these words used to control or demonstrate power? Do we speak to our colleagues or with them? Do we speak *to* our family or *with* them? Consider how *to* and *with* create very different dynamics. *To* requires or promotes:
- Justification
- Self-centered behavior
- Direction
- Control
- Defined boundaries
- Resentment

With requires and allows:
- Co-active behavior
- Ambiguity
- Cooperation and co-activity
- Desired mutual objectives
- Independent thinking
- Co-authorship
- Potential consensus and positive results based on positive relationship

Lying

It is important to take responsibility for the results of our actions. Presenting false impressions can be a source of conflict. For some it can become an endless river of gas feeding flames of conflict draining the parties involved for years or even decades. It takes new lies to keep the old lies fresh.

Why do we lie? We often fear being judged or being put in a position where we have to justify our decisions, behaviors and comments. Remember a time when we created an impression based on information that was incomplete, reorganized or removed to change the paradigm in the head of the person with whom we were speaking at the time?

We define a lie as presenting any other paradigm, regardless of how minimal the difference, than the one we believe to be true. How is information deleted, removed, reorganized to change the paradigm? How are elements of time manipulated? While these are only a few ways to manipulate the truth, it is important to investigate what our parents and extended family socialized us to believe is the truth.

Does truth mean the entire story? If details, insignificant or not, are left out, has a lie been told? Examine the definition of a lie, above, and determine whether the closest people in our lives view it the same way. If not, why? How does each person's understanding of truth impact the amount of conflict they create for themselves, internalize from the outside world, and regurgitate back into the playing field from which we work, live and spend our free time?

So why do we lie? Sometimes it's because we don't want conflict, or we don't want to be judged or have our desires evaluated. We don't want to feel like we have to convince the other person that our choices are appropriate. We do not want to spend the time, effort or work to make communication effective, often because we were never taught the skills. We don't want guilt, more confrontation, frustration and disagreement. We don't want conflict.

Both truth telling and lying are always about choice. We choose to own the consequences and ripple effect that result from a false word, thought or behavior. Even if we do not want to be judged or have to justify our legitimate feelings to each other, we still make a choice when asked to tell the truth or when we are expected to fill in the details. Each conscious thought, spoken word and behavior is ultimately our own to choose and live.

Communication Litmus Test™ [6]

Most of us can recall the middle school science class where we put a strip of paper into a jar of liquid and it turned a particular color to tell us if it was either "A" or "B." Obviously, understanding the chemical aspects of the liquid in the jar would help us determine what it was, what function it could serve and what we could do with the information. The test was intended to provide feedback that we could use as a test or gauge.

When we go game fishing, tossing food into the water (we call it chumming) will hopefully produce the fish we want to catch. In the world of military tactics, it is called probing—an exploratory action, such as an expedition sending troops in one direction to draw a response that can then be used to gauge another's intent, strength and composition. The critical data we send out can be either real or artificial.

This Communication Litmus Test™ stems directly from these concepts and others like them. It produces more than an either/or response; in fact, it can deliver real time data that can be fairly deep and complex. We find it in verbal communication, non-verbal body language and many other forms, even energy or a heart rate that we can sense. What we can gain from this litmus test can be more real and closer to the truth than we could otherwise decipher. The very acts mentioned result in unabridged and uncensored reactions—real data.

Communicating this way allows us to test the ambiguity in a relationship at any given time by delivering pre-determined body language and words based upon previously outlined plans of engagement. In short, we deliver a bundle of information and then evaluate and calculate the response, thus building the basis for our next move. Using communication at this high level allows us to design a customized, real time hybrid outcome based upon pre-designed assumptions, real data and new information.

Often we are concerned about where we stand in a relationship, on a project team, or in a professional or personal relationship. "Paralysis by analysis" can set in; we may feel uncomfortable with the ambiguity or we may even wonder how we are being viewed by this person, entirely.

In these instances, it may be helpful to use the Communication Litmus Test™ to ease our fears or help us move toward a solution. We are using precise language and delivery means to gather data to implement our strategy. That delivery is the calculated inner and outer physiological response based upon how we believe this individual will react to any of the array of our responses, most of which we have planned for in advance.

In essence, this is a planned (yet impromptu in appearance), relationship litmus test that allows us to gather more data in order to understand the physiological and energetic response to contact. Then we can reduce ambiguity around an issue or the relationship as a whole and take appropriate action.

Asking Permission

It is vitally important to ask people's permission to share a thought, offer feedback or ask a question. This demonstrates a respect for their boundaries, time, schedules, emotions, and desire to be open.

Using this technique quickly changes the dynamic of a conversation. Most people do not ask for permission; they just start talking. Consider how many times people gave us feedback or tried to ask a probing question about our logic, and we wanted to scream, "I did not ask you for your opinion!" Well, when we ask, "May I offer an opinion, ask a question about that or provide some feedback?" people do not want to scream. In fact, most are surprised and give permission.

Once they have opened the door, we must be careful with how we frame our question, the non-verbal cues we send and the intensity we deliver with when following up.

Brainstorming

This is an exercise that generates as many options as possible to address an issue or problem. It is critically important not to evaluate any of the suggestions while creating the list. The evaluation process slows everything down and redirects energy and focus while opening up opportunity for judgment and changes in participation level.

The facilitator of the brainstorm should be very careful to ensure neutrality, in both words and deeds. To say, "That's a good idea" after one participant speaks may entice others to question their own comments, their worth, and ultimately the value of participating. Likewise, body language, even when intended to be supportive, can be damaging to the group. It is not acceptable to damage the group or team so that an individual can feel praise or be validated while brainstorming.

General encouragement, however, is valuable and can be used to motivate the group, stimulate thinking and get more out of individuals than originally thought. Asking for "three more" not only builds the list, it builds the relationships. That request also sends the message that the leader of the brainstorm believed in the group's ability to press beyond their limits. What a good analogy to so many other issues related to conflict!

Clarifying

If we were to ask 50 adults the difference between sexual harassment and flirting, we would get 50 different answers. Similarly, what happens when we say that we want respect? What does that mean or look like?

It is important to clarify or get specific about what exactly each person truly means, even if it takes time to get all the information. Both parties must understand not only the words being used, but the specific definition of the words. This puts people on the same page.

Framing

This is a concept that describes how one person verbally presents an issue. It involves immediate attention to the other party's needs. This may be one of the most powerful tools and individual can use when trying to meet his or her own needs or when building relationships or managing conflict.

A framed opening statement in an office communication might sound like this: "I know that we have gotten off to a rough start, but I respect you as my boss, and I am glad that we are going to work this out." It may be necessary to make an educated assumption about the other person's needs, but the important point is the effort made.

We can plan the first words we wish to use based upon an understanding or educated (loosely held) assumption about the other person's needs in the situation, whether we consider them to be valid or not.

If we can get the other person to physically and emotionally exhale, we can help him or her disarm and release the tension that often surrounds communication on difficult subjects.

Re-Framing

Unlike framing, this concept requires two people. When Party A makes a statement, Party B can use different language and reflect the concepts back in a way that is more suited to meeting Parting B's underlying needs. Here's an example:

Statement: "I would like a raise."

Re-frame: "I realize that you would like a raise. Are there things besides money that we can offer you that would satisfy your needs?"

Another set of words is also critical to our overall understanding and conflict fluency. With permission from www.knowconflict.com, they are defined in Appendix A and are useful for better understanding conflict. These help us examine critical aspects of conflict that cannot be expanded upon in this book.

6 Dave Gerber, M.Ed. and Dave Maurer, PMP.

The limits of my language
mean the limits of my world.

- Ludwig Wittgenstein

III.
Who is Responsible?
The Contributing Agents of Conflict
and Socialization

"Personality and socialization aren't the same thing."
– STEVEN PINKER

Social learning is the collective process of piecing together how we should be in the world. The socialization process opens the door to a world of understanding about the ways in which people make decisions, why they behave in certain ways and how they view conflict.

To simplify, it is the ongoing process, starting at birth, of being influenced by the Agents of Socialization: family, media, peers, school and religion.

It is not until we become more conscious of the influences on our being that we truly understand who we are, where we came from and the society we created and live in together. The positive, motivating upside is that after we know this, we can take more responsibility for our decisions to engage or not engage in conflict. We can become empowered to change, to create something better.

Our society has created and passed on formal and informal standards, messages, beliefs and socialization. Early in our lives the Agents of Socialization foster belief systems, positive and negative, that in many cases only work as theories on paper. These are often created to reduce social conflict, keep order and funnel power to the powerful.

Agents of Socialization have affected us throughout our lives. Many of our conscious decisions are truly products of experiences with these five agents over time, particularly from our early childhood. A person's age, parallel life experiences and repetition of events will often gauge which Agents influence him or her at any give time. Most would consider family, particularly parents, to be the primary socialization agent. "The apple doesn't fall far from the tree."

In many ways, we are products of what has been done to us. Social learning and lessons passed along, many with the best of intentions, have influenced all of us in almost all areas of our lives.

Consider the examples below to gain more experience understanding the impact United States Agents of Socialization have on all of us and as individuals. What messages did we get (note the question marks), and how were we socialized by the Agents in the chart? What messages about those topics did we internalize from the Agents of Socialization column, and, quite possibly, pass on to a younger generation?

Replace the question marks with messages from our lives. Remember, individuals from different cultures and subcultures often received different messages about the same concept, group of information or set of peoples.

	Gender	Race	Class	Conflict	Violence
Family	Ex. Women do the dishes	?	Ex. Keeping up with the Joneses	Ex. Parenting style	Ex. Domestic abuse
Peers	?	Ex. Spend time with members of same race	?	?	?
Media	?	?	Ex. Money buys happiness	?	Ex. Violent video games
School	Ex. Men are better at math and science	?	?	Ex. Bullying and cyber-bullying	?
Religion	?	Ex. No inter-marriage	?	?	Ex. War over religion

Listed below are Socialization Questions to think about with respect to the chart. It is beneficial to the true learning of our past to stop reading, substitute the question marks and consider the thoughts on the next page. If we are unwilling to take 30 minutes to consider a lifetime of historical, social learning experiences, particularly from our youth, how can we move forward?

1. Given our experiences, what's behind the question marks in the above table? How did these messages shape our learning, values and life choices?

2. What subtle and obvious lessons or messages did we receive from any of the Agents listed above? Which messages were taught or reinforced with others, particularly to children?

3. How, why and to what extent do we perpetuate subtle or overt lessons passed along by our parents and older generations? In particular, which ones do we pass along that we truly do not support?

4. What other messages did the above listed Agents provide and reinforce throughout our childhoods, adolescence and adulthood?

5. What can be learned from our personal histories? What should we do about it?

6. Is there anyone to discuss this chart and personal experiences with at this time?

7. How would our responses differ from our parents, partner, family, friends and/or colleagues?

"Difficulties are meant to rouse, not discourage.
The human spirit is to grow strong by conflict."
– WILLIAM ELLERY CHANNING

I found one day in school a boy of medium size ill-treating a smaller boy. I expostulated, but he replied: "The bigs hit me, so I hit the babies; that's fair."

In these words he epitomized the history of the human race.

- Bertrand Russell

IV.
F.A.C.T.S.™

"We have met the enemy, and he is us."
– WALT KELLY

FEAR * ANGER * CONTROL * TRUST * SYNERGY

Fear, anger, control, the lack of trust and synergy are the greatest inhibitors to a personal and professional life with reduced conflict. Before explaining each concept in its own individual chapter, it would help to examine some overview questions on the subject.

Use the Agents of Socialization, the Essential Questions and our past experiences to explore each of these concepts and how they are directly relate to us.

F = Fear

- Who would I be if I were not afraid? What could I do?
- What is my approach toward handling fear?
  What fears have I overcome?
- What am I truly afraid of in this life? What can I do now?
- Who can help me overcome this fear?
- What will happen if I do not overcome this fear?

A = Anger

- What is the distinction between disappointed, frustrated and angry?
- How did I learn to be angry and show it?
- Why is anger an acceptable emotion for me?
- How can I anticipate anger before it happens, and what can I do about it?
- What about anger is unacceptable for me?

C = Control

- How does control show up in my most intimate relationships? Acquaintances? Friends? Colleagues?
- Are there any specific control issues to investigate?
- How can I relinquish the need for control in the moment? Is there a way to remind myself when I feel this pull?
- How do I respond when I feel someone is trying to control me in a way that does not damage the relationship?
- How can I manage situations so that it does not look controlling?

T = Trust

- What were my earliest messages about trust?
- What does trust mean to me? Is it a top currency of mine?
- How do I build and sustain trust with friends, family, colleagues and others?
- With whom can I reestablish trust right now?
- What would happen if I went out of my way to demonstrate trust?

S = Synergy

- How well do I work with others? Where did I learn how to be myself in a group?
- What is about others that gets in my way?
- How do I respond to attempts at being included or not included?
- What is the cost of not creating synergy?
- How can I create and demonstrate more value when I am working with others?

F.A.C.T.S. summarizes some of the most basic life issues and obstacles. The timing of our actions and reactions will often influence the impact of a situation. Unfortunately, many people react with conflict or behavior that brings about conflict secondarily.

The fibers of all things have their tension and are strained like the strings of an instrument.

- Henry David Thoreau

V.
F.E.A.R.™

"I must not fear. Fear is the mind-killer. Fear is the little-death that brings total obliteration. I will face my fear. I will permit it to pass over me and through me. And when it has gone past I will turn the inner eye to see its path. Where the fear has gone there will be nothing. Only I will remain."
— FRANK HERBERT

What is fear?

Most dictionaries define fear in relation to feelings of apprehension, calamity, and dread. Experientially, fear has to do with the feeling that something unpleasant or even terrible is going to happen. A moment's reflection shows, however, that fear involves far more than our feelings. It also involves our minds and bodies. A moment's reflection also shows us that there are many levels of fear.[7]

Fear is the mind projecting within itself images of what it does not want to happen. If the fear is not recognized and dealt with early on, it can and will find root within our consciousness. When this happens fear then becomes a daily occurrence, and if these thoughts are allowed to repeat themselves over and over again, they will eventually take an imprint on a subconscious level.[8]

Here is another take on understanding the concept of fear and applying the quotations above—a way to move it from the subconscious to the front of our mind:

Facing – Emotions – Ambiguity – Reality (F.E.A.R.™)

So much of our fear is grounded in past experiences that we dealt with when we didn't have the skills we now possess or are in the process of gaining. This acronym is a good reminder of what we need to consider, fundamentally, when dealing with fear.

First we must confront the fear (**Facing**). It is vitally important that we examine past experiences and make bridges to current behaviors. The only way to deal with a situation, or ambiguity, is to be proactive. The more we use our skills to feel more comfortable, the less likely we are to feel the pain and use our logical minds.

Emotional issues generally have their roots in a prior experience. Whether that is being dropped, hit, spanked or built up, respected and validated, each has a ripple effect through our development. In order to be able to deal with the emotions, we must have the skills to create a bridge between our emotional pain and our logical healing.

When we try to heal issues, there is often a great deal of **ambiguity** around the past experience or recent situation that has taken place. Not knowing outcomes, what skills to apply, consequences, whether it will work or not are just a few concerns that bounce in our heads when trying to deal with the unknown. Being proactive and gaining skills through training, coaching, counseling or a combination will help make it easier to find the courage to want to learn and take ambiguity head on.

That brings us to **reality**, the here and now. Here our truths and the truths of others collide, and we discover how our story differs from what others perceive. Understanding reality as a concept also forces us to think in terms of timelines and/or accountability, from ourselves or others. Ultimately, we have to be the ones that want to improve our daily reality. The only way to do that is to face the painful emotions and situational ambiguity that often brings us back to pain like the crab in the bucket, trying to get out while outside forces make it tough.

Another aspect of what can make this difficult goes back to the old expression, "You can't teach an old dog new tricks." This is not true. It is an enabling excuse for people who want to feel comfortable in the pain (often we can be lazy, too) and not move through the portal to the happiness on the other side.

Pearl S. Buck said, "You can judge your age by the amount of pain you feel when you come in contact with a new idea." Think about being middle aged, doing things the same way for so long. Now we need multiple new ideas to be happier. This is, again, where ambiguity comes back to haunt us. It convinces us that it is okay to know there is more, *but not to go for it*. This is unfortunate. It perpetuates issues and unhappiness in future generations.

The F.E.A.R.™ acronym is a good way to remember what fear is. It's a quick reminder that we have the ability to get over the fear if we choose to do so. Much of our fear is grounded in the unknown. When we become more comfortable dealing with the unknown, we are more flexible, agile and prepared to hear and experience situations with a more confident perspective.

If we are honest with ourselves and sit in a quiet place, center our bodies and minds and begin to think about the impact of fear in our lives, we see many things.
- How many people have we not asked a certain question?
- What have we really wanted to do but always found an excuse not to do?
- When was the last time we had a bold, fierce, collaborative discussion with someone we cared about at home or work?
- When was the last time we said what we really thought at a meeting or family dinner?

Fear is an underlying, baseline, deeply-rooted and, in fact, fed animal inside every one of us. The key to any particular fear, in any given situation is already known at a deeper level of the mind. It often requires the work of a coach to help bring it out of someone. That said, if we can pose to ourselves good questions that we cannot dodge, we will reveal vast amounts of data in the form of past and present feelings, thoughts, desires, fears, goals, and communication styles.

Dorothy Thompson once said, "There is nothing to fear except the persistent refusal to find the truth, the persistent refusal to analyze the cause of happenings."[9] This does not mean that we should spend all of our time in the past. But an inability to understand our parents, socialization process and where our issues come from will ultimately block our ability to grow, find true freedom and happiness, and live out our potential.

To that point, Don Miguel Ruiz said, "Death is not the biggest fear we have; our biggest fear is taking the risk to be alive—the risk to be alive and express what we really are."[10] We must move through the "pain portal" in order to realize the power on the other side.

"Ultimately, we know deeply the other side of every fear is a freedom."
— MARILYN FERGUSON

Regardless of our desirable pursuit of this freedom, fear is something that every human being experiences at some level, like it or not, admit it or not.

Where does fear come from? Do issues from the past (often imposed on us at the time) or the concern about something that has not yet materialized prevent us from moving forward? In true living and learning mode, there is no time for fear. We are too busy living in the moment, ensuring our assumptions and perspectives do not create artificial and unnecessary fear.

Fear is not always bad. Whether a feeling of minor apprehension or absolute terror, fear helps us make associations that protect us from harm. Fear learning is quick, powerful and long lasting. If we think back to our childhood, chances are good that within our earliest memory are events colored by fear. What experiences of fear can we remember that still affect us today?

Who would we be if we were not afraid?

We live in a fear-based society. Think about the products we are sold— tires to protect babies, deodorant to keep us from being offensive, make-up to take away imperfections. The list goes on and on. Consider how many advertisements in this society try to get us to be afraid of something in order to see more value in their product. Unfortunately in the U. S., that mentality has permeated our collective unconscious. We walk around with a generalized sense of fear—a fear of reflection.

What kind of fears do people face? After countless brainstorms and introspective sessions with many people, we believe the following represent many people's common fears.

- *Rejection*
- *Public speaking*
- *Disapproval*
- Taking airplane trips
- *Not meeting expectations*
- Dogs
- Darkness
- Seeing someone bleed
- *Test taking*
- Dentists, doctors and hospitals
- *Making mistakes*
- People displaying anger
- Injections
- Spiders
- *Being late*
- Drowning
- Dying young
- Police
- Growing old alone

While many would think that spiders or needles or dogs would dominate the list, consider the ones that resonate with internal conflict and how common they are with people in our society. The items in *italics* all relate to the fear of being judged. We do not want to have to explain ourselves or measure up to someone else's arbitrary, personal standards that, in fact, may have huge consequences on our lives and happiness.

Fear is a choice. Are we living in the moment and feeling afraid of what is actually taking place in our lives? Are we consumed by rules we have made up about a possible or potential situation that has not even surfaced yet? How often do people stress themselves out, some to the point of physical detriment, merely in the anticipation of an event or potential situation?

When the event happens and goes smoothly, it indicates that the original fear and stress was merely a waste and a strain on our minds and bodies.

Fear inhibits our ability to learn. How often do we let fear get in the way of meeting someone new, trying a new food, changing a standard way of doing something, changing a professional career, standing up for our individual rights, or admitting wrongdoing? When someone truly believes he or she is in a life-long learning mode, there is no such thing as failure, even in the face of risks for which we must build our own safety net.

Fear of something that cannot harm us serves no purpose other than to create chaos and slow us down. This has been described as delusions—distorted ways of looking at ourselves and the world around us. Being in the moment, therefore, is a clear indicator that we have become the masters of our minds, rather than having our minds master us.

We know that certain brain chemistry impacts the way this system works and that genetics are involved. But we also know through studies and personal experience that simply thinking differently and relating differently with the object of our fear can influence the triggering of these primitive brain systems. In other words, studies suggest that we can override some of the primitive behaviors if we create new, learned, conditioned responses.

How to Deal with Fear

1. If possible, plan, prepare and increase our knowledge.
2. Face it. Breathe.
3. Acknowledge the ongoing physiological changes.
4. Take another deep breath, in through the nose, out through the mouth.
5. Replace it with learning, curiosity, and risk taking.
   Our reality test is, "What would happen if it came true?"
6. Remind ourselves that the experience will end before long.
7. Incorporate the information for transformation.
   True learning mode means failure cannot exist.
8. Repeat the cycle and strive for new things now that
   we have moved past old fears.

7   Dennis Lewis, "Transforming Fear," *Authentic Breathing Resources, LLC, n.d.*,
    <http://www.authentic-breathing.com/transforming_fear.htm> (May 3, 2007).

8   John Kehoe, "Understanding Fear," *Learn Mind Power*, August 2004,
    <http://www.learnmindpower.com/Pages/understanding-fear.html> (May 3, 2007).

9   Dorothy Thompson, n.d., <http://thinkexist.com/quotes/dorothy_thompson> October 1, 2007.

10 Don Miguel Ruiz, n.d., <http://thinkexist.com/quotation/
    life-is-like-dancing-if-we-have-a-big-floor-many/374876.html> (October 1, 2007).

**If you are not able
to calm your fears,
your fears will take over.**

- Wes Skiles, Underwater Cave Diver

VI.
A.N.G.E.R.™

"Holding on to anger is like grasping a hot coal
with the intent of throwing it at someone else;
you are the one who gets burned."
– SIDDHARTA

What is anger?

Anger is "an emotional state that varies in intensity from mild irritation to intense fury and rage," says Charles Spielberger, Ph.D. in a brochure published by the American Psychological Association.[11]

Often there are mental and biological changes. If we get mad, our heart rates, blood pressure, adrenaline levels and energy hormones all start to rise. Anger comes from deep inside and can take many forms, especially if it has been suppressed over time.

When someone is using anger as a survival tool, crutch or implement of control, he or she may become negative, quick-fused, judgmental, disapproving, passively resistant, resentful, uncooperative, cynical, unsympathetic, irritable, jealous, unforgiving and argumentative. Before moving on, we must ask ourselves if some of these behaviors even subtly apply to us. The anger will not go away until we explore it, as painful as that may be. But it is worth the short term pain to get long term gain.

When we are angry we often fail to comprehend the truth regarding the real source of the emotion: The initial agitation is only the scab to a similar internal, much deeper pain in our lives. We need to consider more than the event that took us to that place.

The situation that causes anger opens us to a deeper, unresolved issue. Whether we like it or not, that pain may be a reflection of an unmet childhood need, a pressing issue that we are not dealing with beyond the subconscious mind or something we have been dreading or painfully wrestling with during our waking hours.

The instinctive, natural way to express anger is to respond aggressively. Anger is a natural, adaptive response to threats; it inspires powerful, often aggressive, feelings and behaviors, which allow us to fight and to defend ourselves when we are attacked. A certain amount of anger, therefore, is necessary to our survival.

On the other hand, we can't physically lash out at every person or object that irritates or annoys us; laws, social norms, and common sense place limits on how far our anger can take us.[12]

<u>A</u>ccessing – <u>N</u>egativity – <u>G</u>rounded (in an) – <u>E</u>motional – <u>R</u>esponse (A.N.G.E.R.™)

Consider this acronym (Accessing Negativity Grounded in an Emotional Response) and use it as an indicator light when feelings of anger emerge. Internalizing anger may not be the best option. When the light goes on, this will tell us that we need to take more time to respond, behave or speak. If we do not, we are likely to say or do something that will have negative consequences, many of which we did not consider.

Managing our anger can reduce the associated emotional feelings and physiological stimulation most often detrimental to the situation or relationships involved. A key to anger management is the core belief that we cannot change other people or their behaviors. We can only control our responses to them, even when they change quickly.

Trigger thoughts are thoughts that automatically enter your head and trigger certain emotions. This can happen with any emotion, but anger is particularly vulnerable to triggering. For example, if you see people across the room laughing and looking in your direction, you may think, "Those people are ridiculing me!" This could lead to angry feelings, which could lead to retaliatory behavior.

The key point about trigger thoughts is that may escalate an angry situation without any basis in reality. It is important that we try to recognize our trigger thoughts, so that we can step back and assess how accurate they are. In this way we can halt any escalating event that may lead to intense feelings that are difficult to control.[13]

Another key is to know what to do with ourselves when anger arises— to find calm and focus on our breathing. In this state we can control our internal responses and transition to logic and the ability to express ourselves. Eventually we will be able to prevent the destructive feelings anger creates within us.

Someone once said, "I don't have to attend every argument I'm invited to."[14] Not only do we not need to engage with someone's anger (causing it to escalate), we also do not need to have anger be an emotion we allow ourselves to experience. While this may seem lofty, it is a goal we should all incorporate into our lives, because it makes sense physiologically.

If we need a current example to put this into perspective and make it real, consider what William J. Cromie's study reveals about the impact of the anger:

Think about this the next time someone cuts you off in a grocery store line: Anger can bring on a heart attack or stroke. That's the conclusion of several studies at Harvard Medical School and elsewhere. One study of 1,305 men with an average age of 62 revealed that the angriest men were three times more likely to develop heart disease than the most placid ones...excessive ire can take a toll at any age. Researchers at Johns Hopkins School of Medicine tracked 1,055 medical students for 36 years. Compared with cooler heads, the hotheads were six times more likely to suffer heart attacks by age 55 and three times more likely to develop any form of heart or blood vessel disease.

The conclusion is clear: Anger is bad for you at any age. "Among young adults, it's a predictor of premature heart disease later in life," says Harvey Simon, an associate professor of medicine at Harvard Medical School.[15]

Anger can be such a powerful force in our lives that we physically take it out on ourselves. When we get really angry or fearful, we must understand that the body is going through something known as an *adrenaline dump*. When the body senses anger or aggression, it receives a large shot of adrenaline.

While this is normal, it often happens without us knowing it, feeling it, or preparing ourselves to deal with it. The impact of the adrenaline dump cannot be stopped by even most experienced conflict masters. So many people choose to suppress it instead, internalizing the anger. They often project or transfer it onto other people in the form of outward judgments, sarcasm, put downs and maybe even violence.

How to Deal with Anger

1. Limit exposure to people and behaviors that may activate our anger.
2. Mentally recognize anger, identify feelings and don't react.
3. Breathe from the gut!
4. Whisper, "Relax" in our heads, count, do something that works to reduce our heart rates, breathing and tone of voice.
5. Logically consider, visualize and choose from many behaviors.
6. Change our environment.
7. Consider long term life changes, such as meditation, yoga or physical workouts to help slow down our internal motors.

Anger can also be linked back to fear and the next topic, control. Consider the last time we were angry at someone, even if we were right. Ask ourselves some questions about that situation:
1. Am I afraid that he/she won't understand me?
2. Am I afraid that I will be judged?
3. Am I afraid that I won't get what I want?
4. Am I afraid that I won't get what I need?
5. Am I afraid that I will be controlled?

"We avoid the things that we're afraid of because we think there will be dire consequences if we confront them. But the truly dire consequences in our lives come from avoiding things that we need to learn about or discover."
— SHAKTI GAWAIN

11 John McManamy, "Anger and Depression in Bipolar Disorder," *McMan's Depression and Bipolar Web*, n.d., <http://www.mcmanweb.com/anger.htm> (July 26, 2006).

12 American Psychological Association, "Controlling Anger Before it Controls You," *APA Online*, n.d., <http://www.apa.org/topics/controlanger.html#anger> (4/20/07).

13 University of Massachusetts Lowell Counseling Center, n.d., <http://www.uml.edu/studentservices/counseling/mental_health_information/mental%20health%20concerns/anger.html> (4/20/07).

14 (unknown author).

15 William J. Cromie, "Anger Can Break Your Heart: A Hostile Heart is a Vulnerable Heart," *Harvard Gazette Archives*, n.d., <http://www.news.harvard.edu/gazette/2006/09.21/01-anger.html> (September 7th, 2007).

Resentment is like taking poison
and waiting for the other person
to die.

- Malachy McCourt

I
HATE
EVERYBODY
!!!

VII.
Control

"He who controls others may be powerful,
but he who has mastered himself is mightier still. "
– TAO TE CHING

What is control?

Control is when someone else attempts to exercise power, influence or authority over us, subtly or overtly. Conflict often takes place when we do not feel we can be ourselves, actualize our work, live our values, meet our goals or be our true selves. We experience control every day of our lives. Whether it is driving the speed limit, choosing our destiny or what to have for lunch, we make decisions every day based on control.

This may be the single most important ingredient in the F.A.C.T.S. acronym. If we watch an infant playing on the ground, looking to get into something she shouldn't, watch what happens when she is picked up and placed in the stroller. Most children truly fight being moved without their consent. They kick, squirm, cry, pout and slam their fists. Potentially, we all learn at a very early age to fight back when we feel that anyone is trying to control us, as standard research on the subject suggests, between the ages of seven and 10 months.

Individuals in conflict often digress back to these behaviors and reflect their inner children. As adults, we have vast vocabularies with which to express ourselves. Yet we often find ourselves in struggles where both parties are just dressing up basic, childlike power and control situations.

Even an internalized, false belief around control issues is enough to cause a major fiasco. When we get angry, we attempt to control everything. Think of a funnel. When we are angry, behaviors and communication all funnel to control issues.

An Outside Look

The Locus of Control refers to our ability to place the power of personal influence—how we feel about ourselves and others—in our own hands (internal) or in others' (external).[16] Where possible, we want to convert external to internal.

The Internal Locus of Control exists when we place the control of our personal approval, recognition, acceptance, reinforcement, and affirmation into our own hands. It is up to us to develop our own self-love and self-worth. We can feel valuable, creative, smart, capable and skilled. We do not let those feelings be controlled by others. We are ultimately responsible for our own behaviors, thoughts and feelings.

On the other hand, External Locus of Control exists when we are willing to give other people, places, and things the power to influence our feelings about ourselves.[17]

Control Outside Ourselves

Rotter describes the External Locus of Control as giving other people, places, and things the power to influence our feelings about ourselves. It is related to conflicts that are between us and other people.[18]

Interestingly enough, most of the external conflict we blame on others—stupidity, madness or incompetence—comes back to hurt us internally. We then create new external conflict with others in our lives. Remember the story of the man who got yelled at by his boss, went home and hit his wife, who smacked the kid, who kicked the dog? This was nothing more than a cycle of internal-external conflicts repeating and regenerating, like a violent game of whisper down the lane. Who did the man blame for how he was feeling about himself?

In order to move beyond our issues of control, we must work with others every day of our lives. Control has a lot to do with who decides our outcomes.

The "I am Right" Principle

Some of us are affected by this next control concept at a very deep level. This driving force of needing to be right can lead to fear, fear of failure, self-doubt, self-judgment (often to unrealistic expectations), all too often shame and guilt.

No matter the subject, someone's desire to be right can overtake reality and create anything from unpleasantness to utter havoc with others in the environment. Recognizing the desire to be right as an obstacle is the greatest step toward changing. When we observe ourselves behaving this way, we can understand how this desire to be right affects how we frame expectations, communicate, and deal with ambiguity.

Take, for instance, a situation where a couple has been dating for five years. Both have bright futures. The man sees wonderful potential in his girlfriend to grow, build skills, learn, empower herself, overcome fears, live large. Year after year he waits, and she never actualizes that foreseen potential. As a part of the relationship inertia, they get engaged anyway, but he finally breaks it off. He realizes (after being told by an outsider) that his desire to be right about her has blurred the reality that she might never become that person he wants and expects. He decides not to take more time to see if she can change. The relationship ends.

These feelings truly come back to our desire, at a deep level, to complete the master plan we have for the given situation and to say that it was done the way we knew it should have been implemented. This is also a function of pride and ego, our desire to be successful and competent, and a need to get the job done based upon past performances. In order to stop, or at least slow down, the pattern, this rooted anchor must be examined at a deep level, from many perspectives, using multiple, personal, historical examples. Once we become conscious of setting ourselves and others up by this, we can change.

If this desire to be right is still unclear, imagine this. We feel a growing tension as we think about plans to continue a year-long mentoring relationship with someone that is seemingly not making it. We feel a deep sense of disappointment as we clench our fists, grit our teeth, squint our eyes, and either truly or figuratively pound the table while leaning forward and delivering that message to absolutely no one but ourselves: "I am right, I chose the right person, he will actualize his potential one day, I will not fail, I will push on, I will let comments otherwise go unprocessed, I am right and I know this will work." This translates into many types of behaviors, such as kicking the can down the street or pushing the problem to a new day.

Someone once said that every journey has an end. Our desire to be right can cloud the ability to see the conclusion, even when we know it intuitively. This desire to be right comes from our upbringing, overdone confidence, control, fear, anger, shame, guilt and much more. Each person comes to it through different experiences, so we all should spend the time to see its role in our lives.

Hope vs. Expectation

This is an interesting concept that a wise Indian man explained to several people on a plane. Hope is much different than expectation. Hope is a passive emotion and often makes us feel helpless. But it actually changes the way we view situations and can help us support others to make changes on their own time. Hope allows us to be free, to live apart from others' experiences (and pain) while supporting them with little or no judgment.

Take, for instance, a wife who knows that her husband has great potential to unlock. Removing his internal barriers would allow this man to put that potential into action. She can either hope or expect that he changes. Most of us know that while hope seems endless and without boundaries, expectations can quickly lead to ongoing disappointment, frustration, fear, judgment and much more.

How to Overcome Control Issues

1. Recognize the power struggle.
2. Relinquish power. Simply let go of the desire to be right.
3. Move into the experience and out of expectation.
4. Understand the upcoming cause and effect, and take responsibility for decisions and consequences.
5. Understand physiological changes and avoid power assertion and one-upsmanship.
6. Express empathy, sensitivity and the belief in a solution.
7. Have courage to create the opportunity for a perspective change, dynamic shift or an outcome that was different than the one we had before feeling like we were being controlled.

16 Julian Rotter, "The Social Learning Theory of Julian B. Rotter," California State University, Fullerton Department of Psychology, September 11, 2005, <http://psych.fullerton.edu/jmearns/rotter.htm> (July 26, 2006).

17 Ibid.

18 Ibid.

Ultimately, the only power to which man should aspire is that which he exercises over himself.

- Elie Wiesel

VIII.
Trust

"You may be deceived if you trust too much,
but you will live in torment if you do not trust enough."
– FRANK CRANE

What is trust?

Trust is a feeling of connection that includes honesty, respect, kept promises, and mutual support. It "is both character (who you are) and competence (your strengths and the results you produce). It can be both taught and learned."[19] Trust marks the crossroads of logic and feeling.

The need for trust arises from our *interdependence* with others. We often depend on other people to help us obtain, or at least not to frustrate, the outcomes we value (and they on us). As our interests with others are intertwined, we also must recognize that there is an element of risk involved insofar as we often encounter situations in which we cannot compel the cooperation we seek. Therefore, trust can be very valuable in social interactions. [And] trust has been identified as a key element of successful conflict resolution (including negotiation and mediation)[20]

Building Trust

One of the best ways to achieve a winning life is to build and maintain trust in our relationships. Individuals that truly value trust understand, appreciate and utilize the concepts below. Trust can be delicate and difficult to maintain. Balancing each on the list below takes patience, understanding, empathy, vision, opportunity, risk and desire. We build trust by gaining or increasing the ability to:

- Follow through on commitments.
- Maintain confidences.
- Directly address individuals with whom there is a conflict and not telling uninvolved parties.
- Actively listen.
- Accept others without judgment or question.
- Perform responsibilities with quality and timeliness.
- Seek and consider other perspectives.
- Behave consistently.
- Act in a way that matches expressed values, beliefs, and priorities.
- Openly express goals, intentions, and priorities.
- Share information.
- Show respect for others' viewpoints during disagreements.
- Evaluate plans and ideas in an objective, logical fashion.
- Demonstrate sensitivity and tact.
- Involve others in problem solving and decision making.
- Engage in effective communication.
- Work to solve problems rather than assign blame.
- Give recognition and credit to others when warranted.
- Encourage the open discussion of problems and differences of opinion.
- Demonstrate an openness to be influenced.
- Approach conflict collaboratively.
- Remain non-defensive when met with disagreement.
- Take interpersonal risks when appropriate.[21]

How many times have we heard, "Just trust me" (with all types of punctuation!)? Consider the change in meaning and energy when we substitute the period with a question mark or an exclamation point. How often do people just expect us to trust them? How often do we trust people blindly or with little thought? Quite often. There are many additional aspects to trust, such as:

- Ambiguity
- Vulnerability
- Risk
- Assumptions
- Courage
- Confidence
- Openness
- Empathy
- Creativity
- Trust management (It can go away!)

There can be several impediments to building and maintaining a trusting relationship. It is possible that in existing relationships, where individuals have built trust between one another, people are more likely to take risks and handle setbacks and conflict. But if we break someone's trust, we'll have to overcome one or more of the following sensitive obstacles if we don't want to lose the relationship.

Obstacles to Trust

- Lack of resources (time, money, etc.)
- A perceived untrustworthy act
- Overly competitive environment
- Ego
- Status, rank
- Not advancing interests
- Not demonstrating similar interests
- Lack of consistency
- Not supporting the interests of others when they are absent from our environment

Trust as Currency

As discussed earlier, everyone has something that motivates him or her. For some individuals it may be money, for others it may be validation, respect, or vacation time. If we know the type of currency someone deals in, we will know better how to move forward together. Trust is a type of currency for most people; think of how if feels when someone shares our personal secrets, backstabs us at work or breaks a promise.

19 CoveyLink, "How We Define Trust," n.d., <http://www.coveylink.com/about-coveylink/how-we-define-trust.php> (December 26, 2006).

20 Roy J. Lewicki and Edward C. Tomlinson, "Trust Overview," *Beyond Intractability*, December 2003, <http://www.beyondintractability.org/essay/trust_building/> October 12, 2007.

21 Modified from Robin L. Elledge and Steven L. Phillips, *Team Building for the Future: Beyond the Basics*, Pfeiffer & Co., San Francisco, 1989, p. 71; and Steven L. Phillips and Robin L. Elledge, *Team Building for the Future: Beyond the Basics (The Encyclopedia of Team Activities Set)*, The Team-Building Source Book, Jossey-Bass/Pfeiffer, San Francisco, 1989.

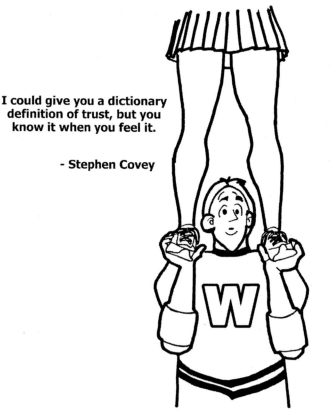

I could give you a dictionary definition of trust, but you know it when you feel it.

- Stephen Covey

IX.
Synergy

"Peace is not the absence of conflict but the presence of creative alternatives for responding to conflict — alternatives to passive or aggressive responses, alternatives to violence."

– LUDWIG WITTGENSTEIN

What is synergy?

Synergy is the linking of factors which each *multiply* the effects of the other(s) rather than simply adding to them. In essence, 3 + 3 = 9. Synergy is the connection of each individual's energy, creating a connection on a higher level. There is synergy when a group of people working together can bring each person's strength to form the group's collective talents and handle conflict as it arises.

Another way to think of this feeling is to imagine another type of "zone" groups get into when functioning at the highest level. Each person is responsible, accountable, delivering at a high level, supportive and dedicated to the overall objectives. People move through conflict and come to solutions more efficiently while meeting everyone's needs.

Why is Synergy Important?

When we consider joint benefits, we know the best results are a product of relationships—the connected energy and efforts of multiple individuals in concert with one another. Some people consider synergy a buzzword. But when we slow down and truly consider the value of synergy, it begs the question, "What am I doing to create synergy in my life, on my teams, in my home?" Synergy represents the ideal, exponential results of multiple forces coming together. Why would we not want that in our personal and professional lives right now?

There are a number of behaviors that we can engage in to create synergy. While we are only responsible for our own behavior, one person modeling successful behavior can influence others. It requires:
- Knowing ourselves and committing to life-long learning
- Respect and trust building
- Effective feedback and communication
- Presence, confidence and humility
- Following words with actions
- Support and accountability
- Leadership skills (We don't have to be the team leader!)
- Relationship building

One of the most difficult aspects of this concept is consistency. Businesses and organizations around the world are spending resources on building high performance teams, managing conflict, providing training opportunities and benefiting from the investment of leadership coaching and team coaching. Why? Because synergy is difficult to create and, most importantly, sustain. Yet it is priceless.

High performing teams, families, and other groups have increased their understanding of how others work and grasped many of the concepts explored in the earlier chapters. "A team is a group of people that uses the collective talents of individuals, a common purpose and collective approach toward a specific set of results while holding each other accountable."[22]

When we understand how we fit into the team, provide value, fulfill our roles, and master fear, anger and control, we increase the group's success rate. To help contribute to the synergy, individuals might ask themselves a few questions:

- What is my purpose for being on this team?
- What value do I bring to the group?
- Can I succinctly share past experiences that demonstrate competency?
- How do I help the team focus on purpose and collaboration?
- How can I contribute to motivating myself and others?
- How can I be clear on the team goals?
- How can I support new group members and demonstrate leadership qualities?
- How can I be fully present and honest?
- How can I reduce the amount of judgment I feel towards others?
- How do my physiology and reaction to comments in situations impact others?
- How can I help to maintain my individuality and avoid group think?
- How do I support others when it comes to taking risks?

Creating a goal of group synergy is a positive step. As the world moves toward a more multicultural experience, particularly in the United States, synergy will be more difficult to create, yet more rewarding when achieved.

22 Adapted from Jon Katzenbach and Douglas Smith, *The Wisdom of Teams*, Harvard Business School Press, Boston, 1993.

**The aim of argument,
or of discussion, should not
be victory, but progress.**

- Joseph Joubert

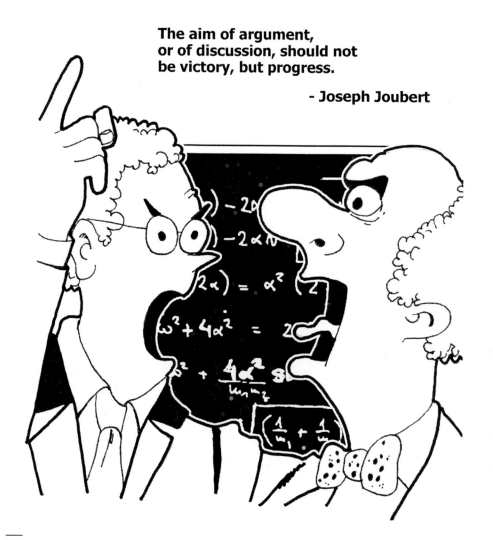

X.
Conclusion

"I think and think for months and years. Ninety-nine times,
the conclusion is false. The hundredth time I am right."
– ALBERT EINSTEIN

Someone once said that "you can blame things on your parents until you're thirty, and then you have to take responsibility." I believe that once we become conscious of how we feel, we make choices. Blaming either ourselves or others really does nothing to move us forward, anyway.

If we choose not to embrace conflict in our lives, we will constantly kick the can of pain down the street, never walking through the portal of pain to increased happiness on the other side. Constant, nagging, draining issues from past experience directly threaten happiness and increased success in the future. Old issues bridge to new issues and make us more sensitive, raising our baseline for stress allowing others to throw us off center. Sometimes this can happen on a daily basis, with or without environmental crisis such as a divorce, death in the family and more.

The tools offered here are intended to be: easy, quick, memorable and helpful with both personal and professional relationships. The true test of self-management is our ability to catch ourselves in the moment and change our emotional states, behavior or language. The sooner we notice and recognize what is going on in our minds, bodies, emotions and even our spirits, the sooner we will be able to release from our judgments, use conflict to unlock our potential, find happiness and advance our winning life!

It does not matter how slowly you go as long as you do not stop.

- Confucius

Appendix A:
A Glossary of Useful Terms for
Managing Conflict

Permission was granted to use the following definitions found at knowconflict.com:

(http://www.knowconflict.com/Impact_of_Terrorv110/glossary.html)

Active Listening - Using techniques to show the other person that his or her interests and concerns have been heard. Active listening includes repetition, reflection, and interest-interpretation.

Aggressiveness - Attempting to get your own way in a dispute by putting physical or verbal pressure on the other person.

Assertiveness - Talking calmly and firmly about your interests and what you want to happen in an effort to communicate effectively with others.

Avoidance - Avoiding a problem by walking away, ignoring what is happening or refusing to participate in a conflict situation. '

Breathe down - Taking deep, slow breaths as a way to calm down and manage strong emotions.

Competition/competitive approach - One side attempts to win and have the other side lose.

Conflict - An uncomfortable internal feeling associated with not getting the things one wants or feeling undecided about what to do in a situation. Conflict is another term for a dispute.

Cooperation/cooperative approach - When using cooperation, people involved in a dispute work together to solve a problem.

De-escalation - Toning down the intensity of the conflict or dispute so that a solution becomes more likely. The angrier people are at each other, the less likely a solution will be reached. The parties can de-escalate the conflict by using good communication skills. De-escalation may also occur when the parties get tired of fighting, or when they realize that keeping the conflict going is doing them more harm than good.

Dialogue - An open, honest discussion between or among the parties in a dispute. In a dialogue, the parties learn about the other's feelings, beliefs, interests and needs, without trying to win over the other side. It often helps to have a third party to facilitate the dialogue so that everyone has an equal chance to share his or her views.

Dispute - The arguments, disagreements and fights that take place between people who are experiencing a conflict.

Disputants - The people, groups or organizations that are in conflict with each other. They are often called "parties." (A "third party" may be a facilitator or mediator who helps resolve the dispute).

Emotion - Another word for feelings. Some common emotions are anger, fear, love, sadness, grief, jealousy, hurt, disappointment and joy. We may have these feelings or emotions in response to things that are going on at the moment or when we remember something that happened in the past. Frequently we also experience physiological changes, such as feeling hot, having our hearts beat faster, changes in breathing, knotting in our stomachs, etc. It is important to separate emotions from the actions we take when we feel something. For example, some people shout or hit when they feel angry. With practice, we can learn to think about what we are feeling and then decide how we want to act.

Escalation - An increase in the intensity of a conflict. When a conflict escalates, the people involved (disputants) move from gently opposing positions to more forceful, confrontational tactics. The number of parties involved may increase, and the number of issues under discussion may grow. Also, when a dispute escalates, the parties may want more than just to win; they may also want to hurt their opponents. Conflict can escalate quickly but may take much longer to calm down, or de-escalate.

Face-saving – One's face is one's public image. When we save face, we avoid making ourselves or others appear foolish or weak. Instead, we find ways to let others appear strong and victorious, even if they are not. People are often concerned that they will "lose face" if they lose in a dispute. If we can ensure that all the parties will save face, an agreement is more likely to be reached.

Facilitation - A third party helps the disputants stay focused on working toward their common goals by following the agreed-upon ground rules. The facilitator takes a less active role in helping the parties find a solution than the mediator would.

Force - Any situation where one party is made to do something they don't want to do because they are threatened with some negative action if they don't do it. Force may be violent, but it can also be a threat to lose one's job or get a bad grade or any other action that is likely to hurt the opponent.

Hate crimes - A crime whose victim is selected because he or she belongs to a group the attacker hates. Some, but not all, hate crimes are acts of terrorism.

Identity - The way we see ourselves. It includes such things as gender, age, nationality, the way we dress, the way we describe ourselves to others, the way we privately think about who we are, and the groups or friends with whom we associate.

Interest-based approach - A type of dispute resolution that looks at problems in terms of interests, not positions, and works to get the parties to understand each other's interests, so everyone is satisfied that their needs have been met.

Interests - The feelings people have about their lives and the reason why they take a certain position. For example, a person may take the position that he will shout back when someone shouts at him, but his interest is to have people talk quietly and respectfully to him. If parties can agree that their interests are compatible they can often reach an agreement, even when their positions are very different.

Intolerance - An unwillingness to accept other people or groups who are different from one's own. When we are intolerant we may want to get rid of the other person, group or idea, or we may just treat them as if they were less valuable or less important than we are. Racial discrimination and prejudice are forms of intolerance.

Needs - We all have basic human physical and psychological needs. These include the need to feel secure, to have a strong sense of personal identity and to be recognized and validated by others. A conflict may involve a demand to meet the human needs of an individual or group. Meeting these needs makes successful resolution of the dispute more likely.

Negotiation - Two or more parties in a dispute discussing a problem intending to find a solution that is acceptable to all. Negotiation can be friendly and cooperative, with both sides seeking a mutually beneficial solution (called win-win, interest-based or cooperative bargaining), or it can be competitive (called win-lose, lose-lose or adversarial bargaining) where one side tries to prevail over the other.

Neutrality - A third party that does not have a connection or previous relationship with any of the parties in the dispute. Neutrality insures that the third party will not be prejudiced toward any of the parties in the dispute by virtue of knowing them currently or in the past. Many mediation programs use a neutral mediator.

Parties - The people or groups involved in the dispute. Third parties are people who are not involved in the dispute but who help resolve it. Mediators, facilitators and judges are third parties in a dispute.

Peace building – A dispute resolution process that involves restoring the normal, cooperative relationship that existed before the dispute. Peace building often involves replacing the conflict with mutual understanding and forgiveness on both sides.

Positions - Each party's stated demand for what they want from the other party. Positions differ from interests, which are the party's deeper needs and wants. Sometimes positions may be opposed to each other, but underlying interests may be compatible. In such cases, the compatible interests may be used as a way to resolve the dispute.

Reconciliation - The return to normal, cooperative relationships between individuals or groups. When parties reconcile, they resolve the dispute. The values of truth, justice, peace and mercy are necessary in order for reconciliation to occur.

Rights - A rights approach to a dispute uses laws, rules, policies or other methods that determine who has the right to do something. The United States operates in a rights system, giving people rights under the law.

Stalemate - Occurs when parties in a dispute are not making progress toward a resolution. Once a stalemate is reached, the parties may be ready for a third party to help them negotiate a settlement.

Stereotyping - Assuming that all members of a group are the same. Stereotyping is dangerous because it oversimplifies the many differences among people of the same group. For example, assuming that all children who grow up in poor neighborhoods will resort to drugs and violence is stereotyping. It may be true of some poor children, but not all. Stereotyping can lead to serious misunderstandings and can hinder the conflict resolution process.

Third Party - A person who helps the disputants resolve their conflict. The third party is impartial and not involved in the conflict. Examples of third parties are mediators, arbitrators, conciliators, facilitators and judges.

Threat - A statement that demands that another party do something, or negative consequences will follow. When a threat is made, one party tries to gain power over the other.

Triggering events - Something that happens to start a conflict. It can be something minor, such as an accidental word or careless mistake, or it can be something major and deliberate.

Value differences - Differences in what people believe and what they consider to be important. People's values are very important to them, and they are usually not willing to change them. Conflicts are often difficult to resolve when the disputant's value differences are great.

Values - Ideas and beliefs about what is good and bad, right and wrong, important or unimportant. We all have values about the way people should behave toward each other in families, as friends and at work. We have values about religion, money, careers and practically every other area of life.

Win-lose (adversarial) approach - Each party in a dispute sees the other party as the enemy, to be defeated. This is contrasted with the win-win approach, in which parties cooperate to find a mutually beneficial and agreeable solution.

Win-win (cooperative, interest-based, or problem-solving) approach - The parties in a dispute work together to cooperatively solve the problem and reach a solution that is satisfactory for everyone. This is contrasted with the win-lose approach, in which each party tries to defeat the other.

Appendix B:
Works Cited and Consulted

In Print:

Fischer, Robert, William Ury, and Patton, Bruce, *Getting to Yes: Negotiating Agreement without Giving In*, Penguin Group, New York, 1981.

Gerber and Leech, *Life without Conflict: Introduction to a Winning Life*, Timeless Publishing, Virginia, 2006.

New World Dictionary of the American Language, 2nd edition, "Fear," Simon and Schuster, Tree of Knowledge, New York, 1984.

Online:

International Institute for Restorative Practices, "What is Restorative Practices," *International Institute for Restorative Practices*, n.d., <http://www.restorativepractices.org/library/whatisrp.html>, (July 26, 2006).

McManamy, John, "Anger and Depression in Bipolar Disorder," *McMan's Depression and Bipolar Web*, n.d., <http://www.mcmanweb.com/anger.htm> (July 26, 2006).

Messina, James J., Ph.D., "Growing Down: Tools for Healing the Inner Child Letting Go of Shame and Guilt," Coping.org, n.d., <http://www.coping.org/innerhealing/shame.htm> 2006.

Panic-attacks.co.uk, "Part 5: The Brain and Panic Attacks: Emotional Hijacking," *The Panic Attack Prevention Program*, 2001-2006, <http://www.panic-attacks.co.uk/panic_attacks_5.htm /> July 26, 2006.

Rotter, Julian, "The Social Learning Theory of Julian B. Rotter," California State University, Fullerton Department of Psychology, September 11, 2005, <http://psych.fullerton.edu/jmearns/rotter.htm> (July 26, 2006).

Wordreference.com, "Conflict," *Wordreference.com*, 2003, <http://www.wordreference.com/definition/conflict/> (July 26, 2006).

Suggested Resources

www.useconflict.com
www.synergydt.com
www.davegerber.info
www.davegerberproducts.com
www.lifewithoutconflict.com
www.kingofconflict.com
www.davegerberspeaks.com
www.onfireleadership.com
www.onfireleaderthoughts.com

How Dave Can Help You and/or Your Next Event

Keynote Speaking
Conflict Management
Leadership and Team Coaching
Workshops, Seminars, Training Sessions
Facilitation, IBN, ADR and Mediation
Conferences and International Conferences

About the Author

*"There is no such thing as a 'self-made' man.
We are made up of thousands of others. Everyone who has ever done a kind
deed for us, or spoken one word of encouragement to us, has entered into the
make-up of our character and of our thoughts, as well as our success."*
— GEORGE BURTON ADAMS

Dave Gerber is President and founder of Synergy Development & Training, llc, an innovative organizational solutions company, that specializes in helping businesses, government agencies, organizations, schools and individuals *use conflict* as an opportunity to increase performance, revenue and reduce risk. SDT accomplishes this through specialized consulting, training, facilitation, conflict management seminars, professional development, leadership and team coaching.

Dave helps individuals understand the impact of conflict at work. He specializes in motivating others to increase and actualize their new professional and personal potential.

Dave has a great understanding of how people work, how to expand upon their possibilities and how to motivate and inspire them to action. He is dedicated to people and relationships. Dave truly enjoys helping diverse work and academic environments prevent, manage and resolve conflict. His expertise spans the areas of conflict resolution and organizational problem solving, team building, group facilitation, Interest-Based Negotiations, diversity education, communication and beyond.

He has worked with business owners, managers, employees of all kinds, CEOs, military officers, business development directors, doctors, lawyers, engineers, educators and more in a coaching, training, speaking and consulting capacity. He has hands-on experience working with thousands of training participants and students of all ages, races, backgrounds and ability levels.

Dave received a Bachelor's Degree in Sociology from Ithaca College (New York), a Master's Degree in Education from St. Joseph's University (Philadelphia), a Senior Executive Leadership certificate as well as a Leadership Coaching (ICF) certificate from Georgetown University (Washington, D.C.). He holds Executive Certificates in Negotiations, Leadership and Management from Notre Dame. He has multiple certificates in Workplace Conflict Processes, Workplace Mediation and Conflict Resolution, Commercial, Federal Workplace and Family Mediation from the Northern Virginia Mediation Service at George Mason. Dave brings 12 years of varied conflict management, teaching, coaching and educator-training experience as well. His passionate and motivating style is contagious.

*"Whenever you're in conflict with someone,
there is one factor that can make the difference between
damaging your relationship and deepening it. That factor is attitude."*
— WILLIAM JAMES

A benchmark of emotional management and responsibility is the realization that our past can no longer be blamed for our actions in the present.

- Doc Childe and Howard Martin